20TH CENTURY fashion

THE 60s

MODS & HIPPIES

For a free color catalog describing Gareth Stevens Publishing's list of high-quality books and multimedia programs, call 1-800-542-2595 (USA) or 1-800-461-9120 (Canada). Gareth Stevens Publishing's Fax: (414) 225-0377.

Library of Congress Cataloging-in-Publication Data available upon request from publisher.
Fax: (414) 225-0377 for the attention of the Publishing Records Department.

ISBN 0-8368-2601-9

This North American edition first published in 2000 by
Gareth Stevens Publishing
1555 North RiverCenter Drive, Suite 201
Milwaukee, Wisconsin 53212 USA

Original edition © 1999 by David West Children's Books. First published in Great Britain in 1999 by Heinemann Library, Halley Court, Jordan Hill, Oxford OX2 8EJ, a division of Reed Educational and Professional Publishing Limited. This U.S. edition © 2000 by Gareth Stevens, Inc. Additional end matter © 2000 by Gareth Stevens, Inc.

Editor: Clare Oliver
Picture Research: Carlotta Cooper/Brooks Krikler Research
Consultant: Helen Reynolds

Gareth Stevens Series Editor: Dorothy L. Gibbs

Photo Credits:
Abbreviations: (t) top, (m) middle, (b) bottom, (l) left, (r) right

Corbis: page 27(mr)
Hulton Getty: Cover (tl, bm), pages 3(tl), 4-5(b), 5(tr, br), 6(tl, br), 7(bl), 8(l), 9(both), 10(t, b), 10-11, 11(tl, tr), 12(mr), 12-13, 13(tr), 14(bl), 16(bl), 19(tl, br), 20(bl), 21(tr, br), 23(r), 24(tl, bl), 26(tl), 26-27, 28(tl, bl), 29(all)
Kobal Collection: pages 20(tl), 25(tr)
NASA: page 12(bl)
Pictorial Press: pages 6(bl), 7(tr), 23(tl)
Redferns: Cover (ml, br), pages 4-5(t), 7(br), 14(r), 14-15, 15(tr), 22(tl, bm), 22-23, 24-25
Irving Solero (Courtesy of The Museum at the Fashion Institute of Technology, New York): pages 14tl, 18tl, 22bl
Frank Spooner Pictures: page 8(r)
© Vogue/Condé Nast Publications Ltd: / Henry Clarke: Cover (bl), page 27(br) /
Duffy: pages 18(bl), 28(r) / Norman Eales: Cover (m), pages 16(tl), 17(br) /
Don Honeyman: pages 20-21 / Horrat: pages 18-19 / Just Jaeckin: page 17(bl) /
Barry Lategan: page 15(br) / Lovi: page 25(br) / David Montgomery: pages 13(br), 17(tl) /
Peter Rand: pages 16(tr), 26(bl) / Jean Loup Sieff: page 15(bl) /
Traeger: page 19(tr) / Justin de Villeneuve: Cover (mr), pages 3(mr), 20(r)

With special thanks to the Picture Library and Syndication Department at *Vogue* Magazine/Condé Nast Publications Ltd.

Printed in Mexico

1 2 3 4 5 6 7 8 9 04 03 02 01 00

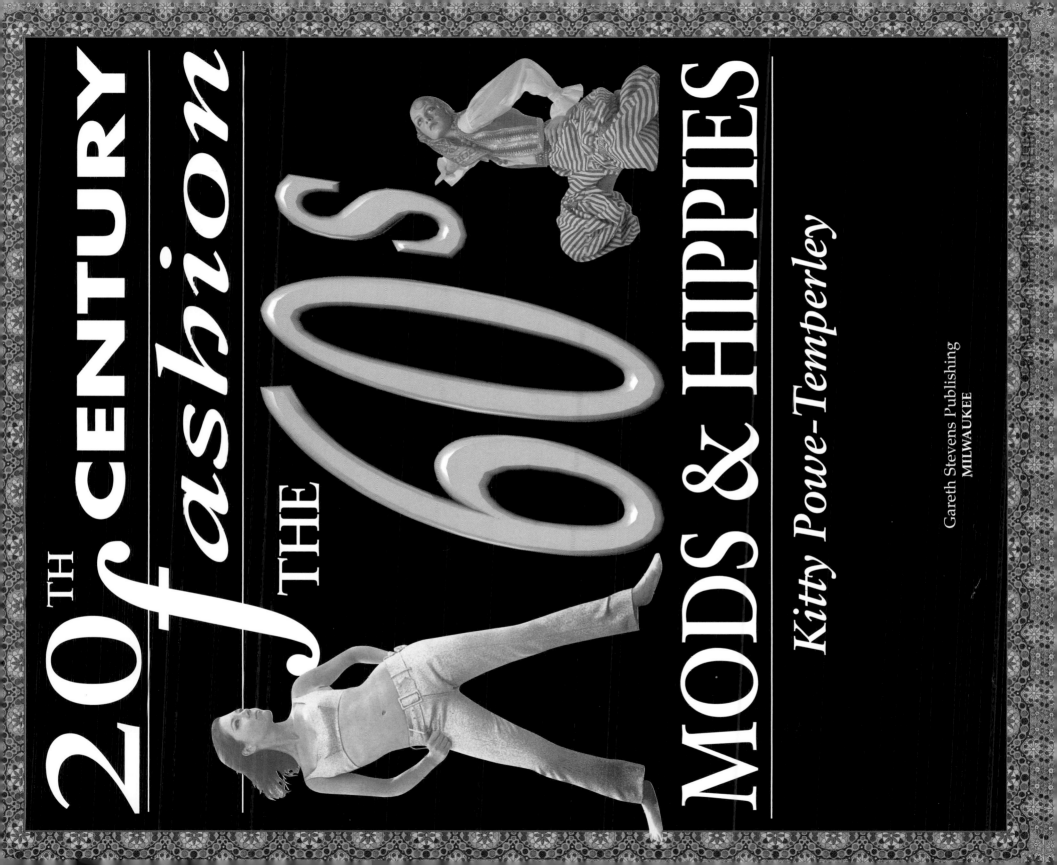

20TH CENTURY fashion

THE 60s

MODS & HIPPIES

Kitty Powe-Temperley

Gareth Stevens Publishing
MILWAUKEE

Contents

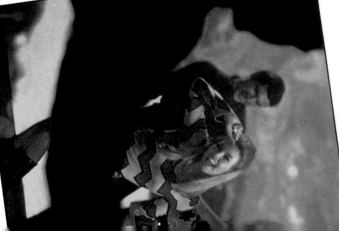

With greater freedom and more money in their pockets, young people set out to have a good time.

The Swinging 1960s

The 1960s might not have been as revolutionary as many at the time supposed, but it was certainly a period of remarkable cultural upheaval. Attitudes toward issues of equality, freedom, and lifestyles, in general, changed forever.

Race riots in the United States and student-led protests against the Vietnam War throughout the West challenged the establishment. After the 1960s, relations between blacks and whites, men and women, governments and citizens would never be the same again.

Meanwhile, new synthetic fabrics, modern production methods, and the rebirth of boutiques made a greater variety of less expensive clothing more accessible to young shoppers. Modern conveniences, such as TVs and cars, finally became available to large sections of society. Television, in particular, was responsible for the influence of popular music on fashion.

In 1960, three years before the Beatles brought their music to the United States, British designer Mary Quant startled Americans by introducing new fashions exclusively for the young. In the years that followed, Paris and Milan were largely ignored — "swinging" London became the capital of the fashion world for almost the entire decade. With the birth of the hippie movement, however, media attention shifted from across the Atlantic to California. The 1960s ended on a hippie note with the largest-ever youth festival at Woodstock in New York.

Pop artist Andy Warhol reflected the new power of consumerism in his work.

The 1960s was a time for demonstrations. Although most were nonviolent, in some, such as the Paris riots of 1968, students faced armed riot police.

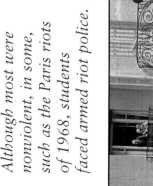

A call to "ban the bomb" was expressed both in demonstrations and through fashion. This dress, for example, features Campaign for Nuclear Disarmament (CND) peace symbols.

Mods and Rockers

To "ton-up" meant to go faster than 100 miles (160 km) per hour on a motorcycle.

While the American "youthquake" rumbled with rockabillies, surfers, and folkies, British teenagers developed their own styles. Some rejected the class-based identity of the 1950s' teddy boys, but still wore suits, adopting a futuristic, international, modern style. They were soon labeled modernists or "mods." Others, clad in leather jackets, continued the biking tradition of the 1950s' ton-up boys. They became known as "rockers."

THE BEST POSSIBLE TASTE

The mods were inspired by the "cool jazz" music of the 1950s, as performed by Miles Davis or the Modern Jazz Quartet. To be *modern* meant to be *minimalist*. For the early mods, the minimalist philosophy, "less is more," entailed a specific dress code: short jackets, drainpipe trousers, polo shirts or turtleneck sweaters, and suede shoes or boots.

Just as no rocker would be seen without his motorcycle, the essential mod accessory was the scooter. Italian makes, such as Lambrettas and Vespas, were firm favorites.

MOD STYLE REVISITED

As the mod movement gained popularity, bands such as The Who and Small Faces, became associated with mod fashion. Mod style evolved further during one of many revivals in the 1980s. Reacting to the scruffy dress of punks, these new mods took on the tailored look of their predecessors, but they developed their own musical tastes. Multi-racial bands, such as The Specials and Madness, borrowed the Caribbean flavors of ska and reggae instead.

The Specials, formed in 1979, wore mod suits.

6

The early mod style was not a matter of who you were or where you came from, but where you were going. Good taste was of supreme importance! Although those who could afford them had custom-made suits, most mods purchased ready-to-wear clothing from chain stores or boutiques.

BORN TO BE WILD

While mods were listening to jazz, *rockers* (a term established by mods) listened to rock 'n' roll artists, such as Elvis and Eddie Cochran. Rocker fashion consisted of studded leather jackets, jeans, and shoes known as winkle pickers. Rockers dismissed the clean, respectable "office dress" of the mods, and mods disliked the scruffy clothes of the rockers.

BRIGHTON ROCK

Rivalry between mods and rockers, most notably in Brighton, England, in 1964, resulted in the rockers' defeat. Never again were they at the forefront of fashion. Their look, however, and their rock 'n' roll philosophy, lived on into the 1990s, inspiring the fashions of headbangers, punks, and psychobillies.

The pop group Small Faces took its name from mod slang, in which face means "fashion leader."

The film Quadrophenia (1979), starring Sting and Toyah Wilcox, dramatized the bitter mod-rocker rivalry during the summer of 1964.

Mod girls liked Quant-style PVC coats in op art, black-and-white, geometric designs, and they wore their hair short and neat.

Chanel Suits and Pillbox Hats

Singer-songwriter Bob Dylan used his lyrics, particularly in "The Times They Are A-Changin'," to define the politics of the generation. He also described one of the classiest fashion items of the decade when he sang "Leopard Skin Pillbox Hat." A stylish accessory for smartly dressed ladies, the pillbox was typically worn to finish off a neat suit, such as the kind created by French designer Coco Chanel (1883–1971).

Coco Chanel designed for comfort, and she wore her own creations. Accessories that finished the look were costume jewelry or chunky pearls and square-toed pumps with a matching gilt-chained handbag.

COCO'S BACK!

Chanel was a big name in fashion during the 1930s. At the start of World War II, she closed her Paris salon and did not reopen it until 1954. Throughout the 1960s, her trademark suits were worn by chic, wealthy women.

FIRST LADY OF FASHION

While Jackie Kennedy was the first lady of the United States (1961–1963), her Chanel-style suits, pillbox hats, and bouffant hairstyle were widely copied. Her clothes were often her own designs, done up for her by Oleg Cassini. When her husband, President John F. Kennedy, was assassinated on November 23, 1963, Jackie's tragic image in her pink Chanel suit and matching pillbox hat was flashed around the world.

Jackie Kennedy and her husband, John F. Kennedy.

SUITS FOR THE SMART SET

The reintroduction of her signature look, a collarless cardigan jacket over a knee-length skirt, made Chanel the most copied designer of the early 1960s. Equally appropriate at a cocktail party or in the office, the Chanel look became a symbol of elegance, whether copied by Oleg Cassini (b. 1913) for Jackie Kennedy or by the home dressmaker. Chanel-style suits are still fashionable today.

Smart suits required smart hair. Here, top hairdresser Vidal Sassoon trims Mary Quant's classic 1960s bob.

THE POPULAR PILLBOX

As in earlier decades, the hat was an essential element of stylish women's dress. Although Chanel often teamed her suits with breton hats (French peasant hats with rolled-up brims), the pillbox was the style adopted by fashionable women, particularly in the United States after New York fashion designer Halston (1932–1990) created one in beige felt for Jackie Kennedy in 1961. The pillbox was designed in 1932 by Hollywood costumer Adrian (1903–1959) for actress Greta Garbo (1905–1990) to wear in the film *As You Desire Me* (1931). A small, oval hat with straight sides and a flat top, it was often made to match the two-piece suit it accented and was usually worn on the back of the head. Its unfussy shape suited most hairstyles, from the bouffant coiffure of the American First Lady to the smart bobs introduced by top London hairdresser Vidal Sassoon (b. 1929).

Mary Quant's "Viva Viva" collection of 1967 was inspired by the contrasting borders that finished off Chanel's suits. Quant's styles and prices made costly looking couture elegance available to a younger market.

Rebirth of the Boutique

The first boutiques had opened in the 1920s. They were small shops within couture houses and sold offshoots from the couturier's line — Patou sportswear, for example, or costume jewelry by Chanel. In the 1960s, however, boutiques took off, specializing in affordable, up-to-the-minute fashions for the youth market.

LONDON LADY

Mary Quant (b. 1934) was ahead of other designers when it came to breaking the hold of traditional made-to-measure tailoring. Her Chelsea boutique, Bazaar, opened in 1955, launching what came to be known as "the London Look." In 1965, *Vogue* proclaimed, "[Quant] blazed a trail, weathered the storm for the young designers." Mary Quant and Bazaar challenged the British retailing system. Clothing and shopping would never be quite the same again.

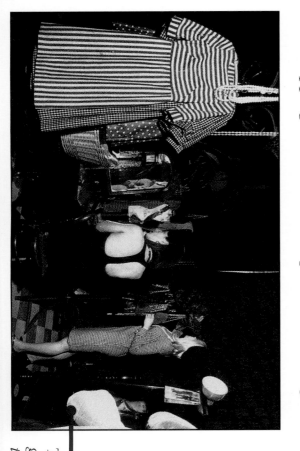

The first Biba boutique, opened by fashion guru Barbara Hulanicki in 1964, was a treasure trove of groovy clothes and accessories.

A customer in a Carnaby Street boutique is trying on an op art suit that features a checked jacket and striped pants.

ALL-AROUND SERVICE

Boutiques offered young shoppers fun clothes, individual attention, and shopping ease that established department stores and chain stores did not. In boutiques, young shoppers did not feel daunted by formalities; a young, trendy staff, hip music, and artistic lighting made them feel at home.

In the summer of 1966, Hung On You was one of London's most "happening" boutiques.

11

SECOND TIME AROUND

Secondhand stores were inexpensive alternatives to boutiques, where people could ignore mainstream fashion in favor of vintage clothing, army surplus, and cast-off designer originals.

I Was Lord Kitchener's Valet was one of the trendy second-hand stores of the 1960s.

A MEETING PLACE

Throughout the 1960s, Carnaby Street was the mecca for adventurous young shoppers in search of swinging London styles. In the United States, San Francisco became the hippie capital. Whether the fashion trend was psychedelic, ethnic, or flower power, boutiques sold what young shoppers were looking for: military-style jackets in bold colors or pastels, flamboyant bell-bottoms, barely-there miniskirts, and tie-dyed T-shirts. Many boutiques sold accessories, too, from space-age plastic rings to strings of ethnic beads. Shops such as Mr. Fish, I Was Lord Kitchener's Valet, and Granny Takes a Trip not only provided merchandise but also offered shoppers a good time looking for it!

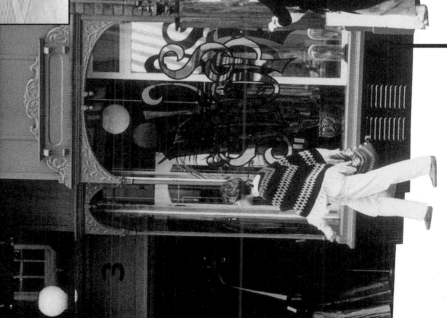

Shop signs in psychedelic lettering reflected what was sold inside.

Space-age Fashion

By 1964, with the space race in full swing, some designers looked to the future for inspiration. Space-age fashions featured sculpted, geometric shapes and exploited the very latest materials, including synthetics, such as PVC, hard plastics, silver Lurex, and even metallic paper.

ONE SMALL STEP FOR ... SCI-FI

In 1961, Russian cosmonaut Yuri Gagarin (1934–1968) made history as the first man in space. Suddenly, space exploration was possible, but no one knew what might be found. There was an explosion of space-based science-fiction comics; TV shows, such as *Star Trek* (1966); and movies. Most of them featured encounters with aliens, and the aliens sparked endless ideas for living — and dressing — alternatives.

MAN ON THE MOON

The 1960s began with a Russian in space and ended with an American on the Moon. On July 19, 1969, Neil Armstrong and Edwin Aldrin landed on the Moon in the lunar module from the spacecraft Apollo 11.

Aldrin leaves the lunar module to take his first steps on the Moon.

ONE GIANT LEAP FOR ... FASHION

In 1964, André Courrèges (b. 1923) presented his "Space Age" collection and captured the spirit of the day. The collection included plastic goggles, astronaut helmets, silver moon boots, and glitzy cat suits. Synthetic textiles gave his designs a sculpted look that was considered "outrageously outer-planetary." His coats, suits, and dresses, with their rounded shoulders and stand-up collars, all had the same profile.

Space-age models pose in silver minidresses and moon boots. (Paris, 1969).

The launch of the Concorde in 1967 made supersonic flight available to non-astronauts! Braniff International saw the connection and sent some crew members to the launch in space-age attire.

Cecil Gee's "Gee-Man" outfit was designed in 1967 with the man-about-space in mind! Most men, however, chose more down-to-Earth styles for everyday wear.

In 1966, Paco Rabanne took new materials to extremes, wiring together plastic or metal tiles to make chain mail.

TO BOLDLY GO

Pierre Cardin (b. 1922) also showed a Space Age collection in 1964. His fabrics were stark white with clear, silver, or black details. Outfits included tubular or A-line jackets worn with slim trousers and short boots and miniskirts worn with mid calf, knee high, or thigh high boots — clothing meant for the adventurous.

A METEORIC IMPACT?

Only a few designers explored futuristic styling for menswear. Cardin was the boldest, adding zippers and pockets to leather or vinyl tunics that were to be worn over trousers tucked into moon boots. Only the ultra fashion-conscious wore them. Cecil Gee's shiny silver "Gee-Man" outfit was more of a publicity stunt than a serious attempt to change the face of menswear! For most women, too, space-age fashions were far too outrageous. Paco Rabanne (b. 1934) was famous for his wild creations in materials such as plastic, paper, and metals, but space-age styles soon changed to a more wearable form. Cardin's slim-cut trousers, for example, went on to become a fashion staple.

The Miniskirt

The miniskirt, at its debut in the mid-1960s, caused a sensation. Hemlines had been creeping up since the early 1960s, but the miniskirt showed more leg than ever before.

SCHOOLGIRL CHIC

Fashion designer Mary Quant is credited with introducing the miniskirt. Following her successful Ginger Group designs, which featured inexpensive separates, Quant continued to present clothing that answered the growing need among teenagers and young adults to freely express themselves.

Like Chanel, Quant designed clothes in which she would look good. Her clothes looked best on women who had a slim, schoolgirl figure like her own. Her long-waisted pinafore dresses with their hip-level belts and pleated or flared skirts stopped just above the knee but looked much shorter than they actually were.

FUTURISTIC STYLES

Quant was not the only designer who was raising hemlines. In the early 1960s, André Courrèges had shown very short skirts worn over tight-fitting trousers.

This baby-doll dress was designed by Courrèges, who claimed to have invented the miniskirt.

The "Breakaway Girl" collection of 1966 featured shorter-than-short nylon minidresses, with pink paisley-print sleeves and tights.

Thigh-high minidresses in sheer fabrics created the baby-doll look.

14

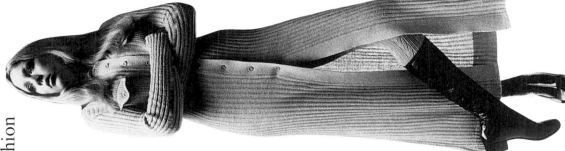

The British mini car (right) was a 1960s classic.

"FREE" STYLE

Newfound freedoms in art, music, fashion, dance, and many other forms of expression led to significantly freer lifestyles, especially for women, teens, and young adults.

The miniskirt gave women a new sense of freedom (left).

By 1965, women were generally wearing miniskirts with mid-calf boots. Courrèges' designs, with their futuristic styling and sharp, angular lines, suited shorter skirt lengths well and made fashion headlines on both sides of the Atlantic.

A-HEM!

By 1967, miniskirts had risen from just above the knee to the mid-thigh and were widely worn by younger women. As the decade drew to a close, designers introduced a variety of skirt lengths, from a very skimpy mini, which barely covered the behind, to a calf-length midi, which usually had an A-line shape and was worn by women of all ages, to the maxi-length coat or skirt, which reached the ankle — or the floor.

In the following decades, women have continued to experiment with skirt lengths, sometimes following a designer's lead but generally choosing the length that best suits their own personal tastes and lifestyles.

The A-line midi was welcomed by women who did not feel comfortable revealing so much leg.

The maxi-coat was often worn over a minidress. Knee-high boots completed the look.

Shoes, Hats, and Accessories

Synthetics such as Corfam provided an easy-care alternative to suede.

As skirts became shorter, more leg came into view, drawing attention to the extremities. Shoes had a more chiseled look and less heel. Flat shoes were perfect with Mary Quant's textured, patterned tights.

Shoes in the 1960s were two-tone or had holes cut out to create interesting patterns. Toes were squarer than in the 1950s.

BEAUTIFUL BOOTS

In the 1960s, boots were no longer treated as an item only to be worn in bad weather. In this decade, boots reached from the ankle to the thigh, and they were popular with all age groups. Calf-high, shiny white boots by André Courrèges had clear, cutout tops and conformed to the silhouette of his space-age clothing. A leather or vinyl knee-high boot, often called a go-go boot, zipped or laced up to fit the leg snugly. The go-go boot remains popular today for both casual and high-style dress.

For men, the look of the early 1960s was ankle-high Chelsea or Beatle boots with stacked heels and pointed toes. Space boots were popular by mid-decade, and, along with cowboy boots, remained essential casual wear well into the 1970s.

This wacky-looking, kid leather balaclava appeared in 1963. It was ultra modern — but warm.

SUMMERTIME SHOES

Hippies of the 1960s, when not going barefoot, were most likely to be wearing simple sandals with two buckled straps.

For the style-conscious, strappy, jewel-encrusted sandals were a breezy alternative to boots and looked good with everything. After 1967, sandals began to appear with higher heels and thicker soles, heralding the platform shoe.

Leg makeup and sparkly sandals were popular when it was too hot for boots and tights.

HAT TRICKS

The bobs and urchin cuts of the early 1960s could be worn with an elegant pillbox or a 1920s-style cloche, but, most often, the head was left bare. Hippies popularized a wide range of headgear. In addition to their famous headbands, they wore huge, floppy sunhats; pointed, wizard-style hats; artsy berets; decadent top hats; and peaked caps. As always, anything went!

A crocheted cloche might be worn with plastic sunglasses, hole-punched gloves, and a two-tone handbag. Mixing patterns, shapes, and textures was fashionable.

STYLE-LASH EYES

The dolly-bird look emphasized the eyes. Multiple coats of mascara achieved its wide-eyed stare until, in 1964, false eyelashes were marketed. At first, each eyelash had to be stuck on individually, but they were soon available as stick-on strips. Black was generally the color of choice, but false eyelashes also came in outrageous golds, silvers, and colored glitters.

False eyelashes were not designed to look natural!

When Art Became Fashion

In the 1960s, the boundaries blurred between art and fashion. Artists, such as Bulgarian-born Christo (b. 1935) and American Mimi Smith, created clothes as works of art, and designers raided pop art and op art for patterns. On canvas or on fabric, the clever use of shapes, such as circles, squares, and spirals, gave the illusion of movement.

Andy Warhol's pop art "soup" paintings found their way from the art gallery to the catwalk.

JUST AN ILLUSION

Op art, or "optical art," became a huge fashion trend. English artist Bridget Riley (b. 1931) was a noted figure in the movement. Her black-and-white circles, zigzags, squares, and rectangles were cleverly repeated to create a 3-D effect; her work seemed to recede, protrude, or ripple.

Vogue provided the op art pattern for this shorts suit. The fabric's strong zigzags seemed to wobble and shift as the wearer walked along.

Some textiles featured built-in illusions, such as moiré-effect velvet (bottom, left) that shimmered and swirled in the light.

Cecil Gee's spring collection for 1966 saw men modeling black-and-white, op art-style leather jackets.

This illusion worked by confusing the optic nerve in the eye. Textile designers jumped at the chance to use the same trick in their fabrics. As a result, designers such as London-based Ossie Clark (1942–1996) and Paris-based Yves Saint Laurent (b. 1936) created fashions that dazzled.

FAKING IT

Trompe l'oeil, a term that means "to fool the eye," was another method used to create a 3-D effect. Translated into fashion, it was used to knit pretend collars or cuffs into the design of a sweater or to give dresses contrasting belts and pockets.

HOMEMADE ART

Tie-dyeing became popular among those who preferred to make their own art. This simple technique enabled even the least artistic to create endless swirling patterns in a rainbow of colors. Although tie-dye remains a hallmark of the 1960s, tie-dyed T-shirts and dresses are still sold nearly forty years later.

Mondrian's paintings were a fashion inspiration, as seen in this striking 1965 cocktail dress.

ABSTRACT ART

In 1965, Yves Saint Laurent based a fashion collection on the work of Dutch artist Piet Mondrian (1872–1944). Mondrian used primary colors, along with white, gray, and black, to create his geometric forms, which were ideal for Saint Laurent's boxy dresses.

Saint Laurent (center) with two models.

19

Icons of Fashion

The link between media, music, and fashion was central to popular culture in the 1960s. James Bond movies and TV shows such as *The Avengers* and *The Man from U.N.C.L.E.* established idols for both males and females. Magazines, such as 'Teen, Teen World, and Teen Screen, aimed primarily at teenage girls, featured rock and film star pinups, along with makeup and fashion tips.

GIRLISH SUPERMODELS

The two most famous models of the decade were Jean Shrimpton and Twiggy. "The Shrimp" was seventeen when she began modeling. Twiggy, whose real name was Lesley Hornby, was just sixteen when she was dubbed "the face of 1966." Twiggy's boyish figure made her the ideal clotheshorse, whether she was modeling simple minis or flowing hippie caftans. Her striking features matched the new taste for wide-eyed innocence.

James Bond movies were firm favorites at the box office, promising thrills, adventure, and the latest fashions.

Twiggy's huge eyes and pouty mouth were a familiar look of the 1960s.

Model Patti Boyd broke millions of hearts by marrying Beatle George Harrison.

AVENGING ANGELS

Television heroines, such as Cathy Gale (played by Honor Blackman) and Emma Peel (played by Diana Rigg) of *The Avengers*, were sophisticated, stylish, and strong. They dressed in skintight black leather or gleaming PVC cat suits.

Model Jean Shrimpton poses amid examples of another style classic of the 1960s — the British mini car!

WOMEN'S LIBBERS

It was no accident that the media portrayed stronger women. The changes of the 1960s were freeing women from their traditional domestic roles. Throughout the decade, women known as feminists fought hard for women's rights. Tired of female stereotypes, especially in the workplace, these women wanted more say and more pay.

Marches kept the issues of women's rights alive.

Although Diana Rigg wore trousers as Emma Peel in The Avengers, she was always a sidekick to the male role, John Steed.

ONE FOR THE BOYS

The media was busy defining roles for men as well as for women. Movies, television, and, particularly, pop music overloaded young men with information about how they should look.

Because this information was available to young women, too, they could compare how their male friends' fashion sense measured up against the popular appeal of Mick Jagger or the sleek sophistication of James Bond!

Young men as well as young women kept a close watch over their images as they found themselves challenged by their peers, and by the media, to conform to every new trend.

Male Followers of Fashion

The mods paved the way for a change in attitude to menswear. For the first time since the 1700s, it was all right for men to be stylish and make an effort to dress well. Men's fashion shifted from the conservative, classic look of a tailored suit to "anything goes." With the Beatle jacket in 1963, the Carnaby Street splendor of the mid-sixties, and the relatively feminine styles that closed the decade, a menswear revolution had occurred.

Mick Jagger, the peacock of pop, struts the stage in a full-sleeved shirt.

PAISLEY POWER

In the 1800s, inspired by the Mughal art of India, the Scottish town of Paisley produced patterned shawls imitating real cashmeres. By the 1960s, paisley covered everything.

Paisley suits for men were not unusual.

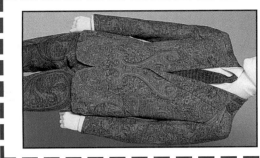

MODS À LA MODE

Thanks to the mods' minimalist look, young men's fashions became more of an expression of individuality. The drab, three-button suit worn by men since the turn of the century was too "establishment." Style-seeking men wanted more choice!

Exploding onto the pop scene in 1963, the "Fab Four" created a fashion craze for copycat Beatle jackets and tight-fitting trousers.

Even men who were lost without a suit became more stylish as the decade wore on.

From head to toe, hip young men created their own "thrown-together" style.

BOUTIQUES FOR BOYS

With more spending power in the 1960s, men no longer needed to buy a wardrobe to last a lifetime. Department stores offered more affordable clothing in a wider range of styles, and new boutiques, such as His Shop and Vince, provided trendy clothing and accessories.

LIKE A RAINBOW

To end the drab and conformist attitudes left over from World War II, colored suits and shirts appeared in London's West End shops. White, pink, cinnamon, and mustard were among the favorites.

The desire to dress to express personality led to increasingly flamboyant styles for men. They escaped their traditional roles by wearing frilled dress shirts, rainbow-colored velvet jeans, hip-hugging trousers, and ethnic, unisex caftans.

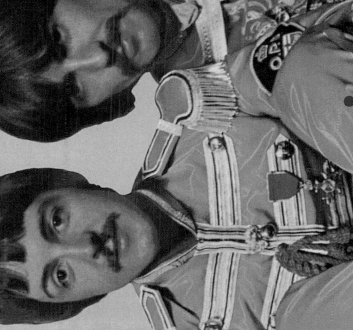

By 1967, when they launched Sgt. Pepper, the Beatles had embraced Indian-inspired music and decadent clothing.

Hippie Styles

The hippie look, one of the many anti-fashion statements of the twentieth century, defined the 1960s. Hippie slogans, such as "Peace" and "Love," reflected the desire to find alternative ways of living in which individuals could drop out of society to focus on their spiritual lives, instead of being slaves to money.

Peaceful protest was the method chosen by most young adults who wanted to make their views known.

BEFORE THE HIPPIES

The hippie movement blossomed in 1965 in the Haight-Ashbury area of San Francisco. It developed from the ideas of those who preceded hippies in anti-establishment lifestyles. Their carefree attitude, for example, came from the beatniks, their hedonism from the surfers, and their political conscience from the folkies.

By 1967, the Beatles were promoting the hippie look — and its spiritual quest. They made a pilgrimage to India and had their own guru, Maharishi Mahesh Yogi (seated, far right).

"Flower power" was about going back to nature. The flower was a symbol of natural beauty.

24

Although motorcyclists often seemed to be the exact opposite of peace-loving hippies, some bikers even attended Woodstock — as bouncers!

HIPPIE CHIC

While long hair, beads, bare feet or sandals, and bell-bottoms are what most people associate with hippie fashion, just about anything was worn as long as it was loose-fitting and ethnic. Women wore shawls and peasant blouses with long skirts made of inexpensive and colorful Indian or African cotton fabrics. Men teamed Eastern-style tunics with embroidered vests and denim jeans or velvet trousers. A non-ethnic version of the hippie look emerged in 1967, at the height of the hippie era. Both men and women wore clothes made of synthetics and other manufactured fibers. Bright patterns, such as paisley and flower designs, complemented the music of the day.

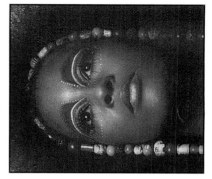

A HUMAN CANVAS
Reacting against drab conformity, hippies used body paint to adorn themselves with brightly colored designs and flower motifs. The wilder the designs, the "groovier."

For hippies, body painting was a means of self-expression.

Eastern Influences

As hippies turned to the East for inspiration, so did fashion designers. At first, the hippie mix-and-match approach to ethnic styles seemed a way to reject Western consumerism. Soon, of course, those back-to-basics caftans were a booming business.

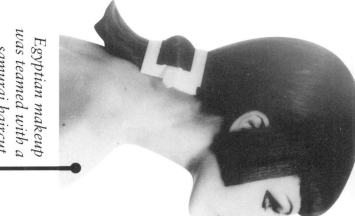

Egyptian makeup was teamed with a samurai haircut.

HIPPIE SHAKE-UP

Detesting conformity, the hippie movement of the late 1960s blended the ethnic with the exotic. The world was the hippie's supermarket, especially the East. Both males and females wore caftans, which were loosely cut, ankle-length garments based on African and Arabic tribal dress. Fibers had to be natural, so caftans were made of cotton, wool, or silk.

For a more tailored look, hippies wore baggy Arabian pants. These flamboyant, sultan-style trousers were made of brightly colored silks and cottons.

BOYS WILL BE GIRLS

At first, ethnic clothes were purchased at small boutiques or by mail order from the mushrooming textile import businesses. Before long, however,

Menswear, 1967-style, included this braid-trimmed woolen caftan designed by Adolpho de Velasco.

26

streetwise fashion designers, such as Ossie Clark, were recreating the hippie look for themselves. By the end of the decade, the caftan had made it to the catwalks of haute couture houses. Wealthy women attended elegant dinners in hand-embroidered caftans of flowing silk.

COMPLETING THE OUTFIT

Exotic accessories included scarfs of raw silk in Indian prints, hand-embroidered vests, and beads — lots of beads! Beads came in polished, semi-precious stones or carved wood and were worn by both men and women in long strings around the neck.

BUILT FOR COMFORT

Eastern styles met the desire for a more spiritual way of living and became the first truly unisex fashions. More practically, these loose, flowing clothes were very comfortable. Designed for wear in countries that could get unbearably hot, there were no tight waistbands, and the sleeves were loose so they did not bind under the arms. Also, this clothing could be worn by people of any shape or size.

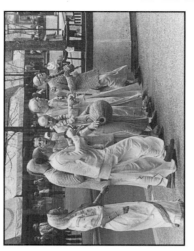

Hare Krishnas shave their heads and wear flowing Hindu robes.

Photographers headed East in search of exotic backdrops. This model is posing in the Taurus Mountains of Turkey.

In 1967, London hosted the first hippie fashion show. Designer Michael Rainey (left) modeled his Arabian cloak, or djellaba. Eija (right) wore a baggy pantaloon suit by Ossie Clark.

The Technology of Fashion

In the 1960s, more than ever before, fashion proclaimed individuality, function, and fun. The development of exciting new synthetic fabrics and the discovery of new ways to use materials such as rayon, nylon, and polyester made it possible.

FUELING FASHION

Du Pont introduced nylon, the first of many synthetic fabrics, in 1938. Under the brand names Terylene and Crimplene, it was widely used in both underwear and outerwear because it was very durable and took colored dyes well.

This "radical" Terylene suit (1967) was designed by Schwartzman of Sweden.

Acrylonitrile is polymerized in a reactor.

Then it is dissolved in a solvent to make it semi-dull.

A filter removes impurities.

The liquid is forced through a spinneret into a bath to form the fiber.

The fiber is drawn through a dryer. Then it moves on to the stretcher, crimper, and baler.

SYNTHETIC STOCKINGS

Mary Quant was one of the first dress designers to design hosiery. She capitalized on the availability of nylon in very fine deniers. In 1965, she made the first patterned stockings with floral sprigs, and, in 1967, she designed nylon tights bearing her daisy logo.

Acrylic fiber is made from a resin that is chemically produced from petroleum.

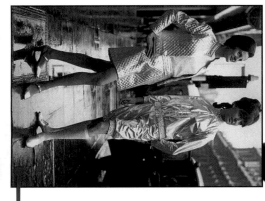

Sparkling Lurex lamé was used to create space-age styles, such as these shorts and knickers.

28

in the 1960s

PRETTY POLLY

Polyester was wrinkle-resistant and quick-drying, and it kept its shape. First used in furnishings, it became one of the most widely used synthetics. Polyester and its derivative, acrylic, were popular with designers under the trade names Dacron and Orlon, for outerwear, and Lycra and Antron, for underwear and swimwear.

THROWAWAY FASHION

Materials such as paper and plastic enjoyed brief popularity during the mid-1960s. PVC (polyvinyl chloride) was a fashionable alternative to leather. It dyed well and suited styles ranging from mod to space-age. Paper that was reinforced with nylon was used, briefly, in suits and underwear, but disposable clothing never became more than a passing trend.

FEET FIRST

Corfam, another Du Pont product, was also developed as a leather substitute. It was soft and supple and, like leather, allowed feet to breathe. Corfam was widely used for boots, especially after Mary Quant used it in her ankle boots. Synthetic materials had a huge impact on 1960s fashions, making them more colorful, more varied, and, most importantly, more affordable.

Designer Daniel Hechter created disposable dresses in 1966.

Designed in 1966, this pantsuit was made from state-of-the-art PVC.

Using aluminum, hole-punched for a dramatic effect, Paco Rabanne updated medieval chain mail for women's wear. This glittering metal minidress (right) is an example of Rabanne's designs.

29

Year	FASHION	WORLD EVENTS	TECHNOLOGY	FAMOUS PEOPLE	ART & MEDIA
1960	•Mary Quant launches designs in U.S. •Valentino's first show	•Belgian Congo granted independence •U.S. nuclear submarine Triton circumnavigates the world underwater	•Laser invented •U.S. nuclear submarine becomes president	•USSR: Leonid Brezhnev becomes president •Madonna born	•Yves Klein: Anthropométries •Alfred Hitchcock: Psycho
1961	•Courrèges opens •Jackie Kennedy appoints Oleg Cassini her official designer	•Bay of Pigs invasion of Cuba •Berlin Wall built •OPEC formed	•Yuri Gagarin is the first man in space •Renault 4 first produced	•Ernest Hemingway commits suicide •Ballet star Nureyev defects from USSR	•Claes Oldenburg opens "The Store," selling plastic replicas of food
1962	•Hardy Amies: menswear •Daniel Hechter opens	•Cuban missile crisis •Algeria gains independence from France	•Telstar satellite launched	•Marilyn Monroe dies •France: Georges Pompidou named Prime Minister	•Warhol: One Hundred Campbell's Soup Cans •Burgess: A Clockwork Orange
1963	•Mary Quant starts "Ginger Group" •Sassoon: "Nancy Kwan" bob	•Nuclear Test Ban Treaty signed by USSR, UK, and USA	•Philips introduces audio cassette tapes	•U.S.: President John F. Kennedy assassinated •Bruce Reynolds leads Great Train Robbery	•Roy Lichtenstein: Wham! •Beach Boys: Surfin' USA
1964	•Courrèges: "Space Age" •Biba opens	•UN sanctions against South Africa •Vietnam War begins	•Word processor invented •Moog synthesizer invented	•Muhammad Ali: world heavyweight champion •Mandela jailed in South Africa	•The Hollies: In the Hollies Style •Goldfinger •A Fistful of Dollars
1965	•Yves Saint Laurent: "Mondrian" dress •Rabanne: plastic dress	•India and Pakistan at war •End of capital punishment in UK •PLO formed	•Completion of France–Italy road tunnel through Mt. Blanc	•Malcolm X assassinated	•Bridget Riley: Arrest I •Doctor Zhivago •The Sound of Music
1966	•Yves Saint Laurent: ready-to-wear •Jean Muir opens •Rabanne: body jewelry	•Cultural revolution in China	•Fuel injection engines for cars introduced in UK	•England's football (soccer) team wins World Cup	•David Hemmings: Blow-Up •Bob Dylan: Blonde on Blonde
1967	•Oscar de la Renta: "Gypsy" collection •Yves Saint Laurent: knickerbocker suit	•Six-Day War between Arabs and Israelis	•First heart transplant in Bolivia •Dolby invents noise reduction system for stereos	•Che Guevara killed in Bolivia •Artists Gilbert and George first meet	•Walt Disney: Jungle Book •Beatles: Sgt. Pepper's Lonely Hearts Club Band •The Doors: The Doors
1968	•Zandra Rhodes opens •Sonia Rykiel opens •Hechter: duffle coats	•USSR invades Czechoslovakia •Student riots in Paris •Vietnam: Tet Offensive	•Aswan Dam completed	•Martin Luther King, Jr. assassinated •Yuri Gagarin dies in plane crash	•Chitty Chitty Bang Bang •2001: A Space Odyssey •Marvin Gaye: I Heard It through the Grapevine
1969	•Rei Kawakubo founds Comme des Garçons •The Gap founded	•Stonewall Uprising: beginning of Gay Rights movement	•Neil Armstrong: first moon walk •Concorde's first flight	•John Lennon and Yoko Ono married •Ronald and Reggie Kray jailed	•U.S.: Woodstock music festival

Glossary

A-line: a shape or style that is narrow at the top and flared at the bottom.

beatniks: followers of a 1950's anti-establishment movement, identified by their unconventional dress and behavior and their strong belief in self-expression.

bell-bottoms: trousers that flare out widely at the bottoms of the legs.

cloche: a close-fitting, 1920s-style, ladies hat with a deep, rounded crown and a very narrow brim.

consumerism: a social system based on the buying and selling of consumer goods.

denier: a unit of measurement that specifies the fineness of yarns, especially silk, rayon, and nylon yarns.

dolly bird: a British term to describe a very young and attractive woman.

folkies: followers of a politically conscious, 1950's movement led primarily by folk singers and musicians.

hedonism: a belief in living only for pleasure.

op art: a style of art that uses straight and curved lines and geometric patterns to create an optical illusion.

paisley: a patterned fabric, originally made in Scotland of soft wool, marked with a characteristic design of colorful, swirling, abstract and floral-like figures.

pop art: a style of art that uses everyday items and objects, such as soup cans and road signs, for its subject matter.

PVC: the abbreviation for "polyvinyl chloride," a synthetic plastic material, one form of which is a shiny vinyl fabric.

tie-dye: a technique for dyeing fabric by knotting it in several places so the color forms a swirling pattern.

unisex: not able to be distinguished as either male or female; suitable for both males and females.

winkle pickers: shoes or boots with long, pointed toes.

More Books to Read

The 1960s. Fashion Sourcebooks (series). John Peacock (Thames and Hudson)

Dressed for the Occasion: What Americans Wore 1620-1970. People's History (series). Brandon Marie Miller (Lerner)

Fashion Model. Fashion World (series). Miriam Moss (Crestwood House)

Fashionable Clothing from the Sears Catalogs — mid 1960s. Joy Shih (Schiffer)

Fashionable Clothing from the Sears Catalogs — late 1960s. Desire Smith (Schiffer)

Fashions of a Decade: The 1960s. Fashions of a Decade (series). Yvonne Connickie (Facts on File)

Fifty Years of Fashion: New Look to Now. Valerie Steele (Yale University Press)

Flower Power: Prints from the 1960s. Tina Skinner (Schiffer)

Great Fashion Designs of the Sixties: Paper Dolls in Full Color. Tom Tierney (Dover)

Op to Pop: Furniture of the 1960s. Cara Greenberg (Bulfinch Press)

Web Sites

Bad Fads: Fashion.
www.badfads.com/fashionframe.html

infoplease.com kids' almanac: Fashion and Dress.
www.kids.infoplease.com/ipka/A0767725.html

Timeline of Costume History.
20th Century Western Costume: 1960-1970
www.costumes.org/pages/timelinepages/1960s1.htm

Virtual Carnaby. *www.carnaby.co.uk/*

Due to the dynamic nature of the Internet, some web sites stay current longer than others. To find additional web sites, use a reliable search engine with one or more of the following keywords: *boots, boutique, caftan, Cardin, Carnaby Street, Cassini, clothing, couture, fashion, flower power, Halston, miniskirt, op art, polyester, Quant,* and *Twiggy*.